This Book
Belongs To

....

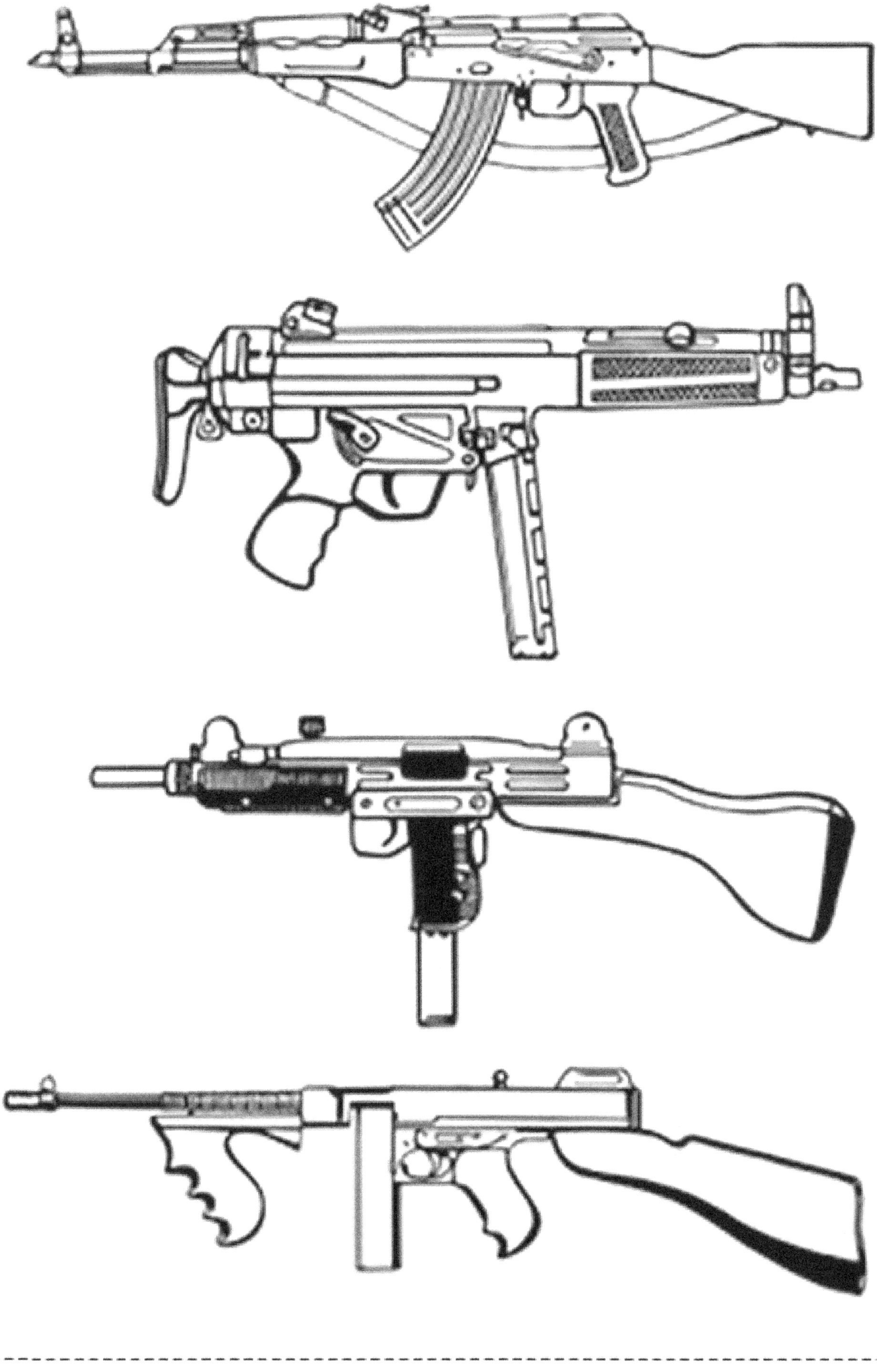

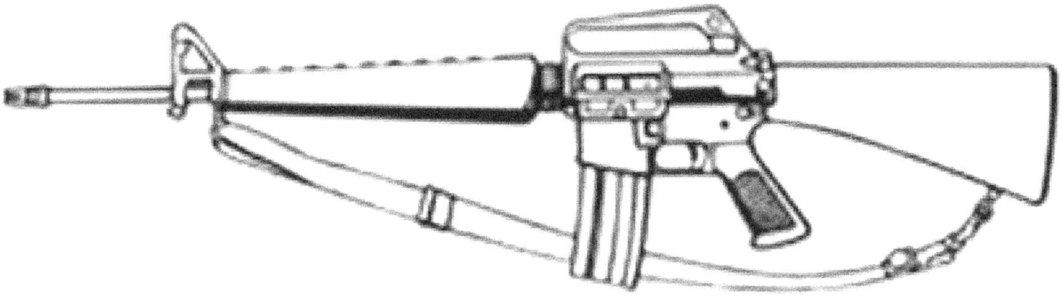

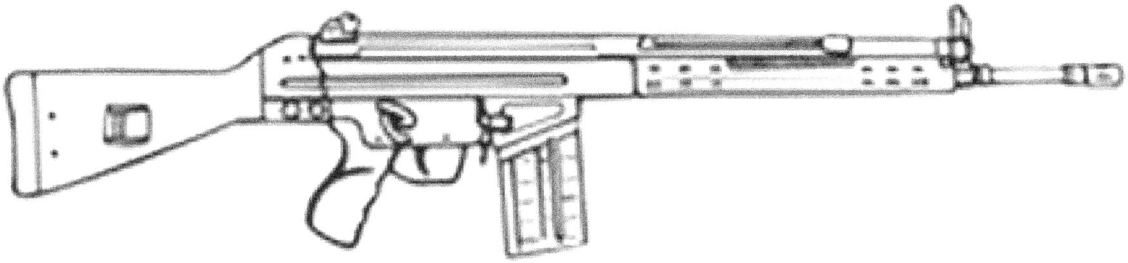

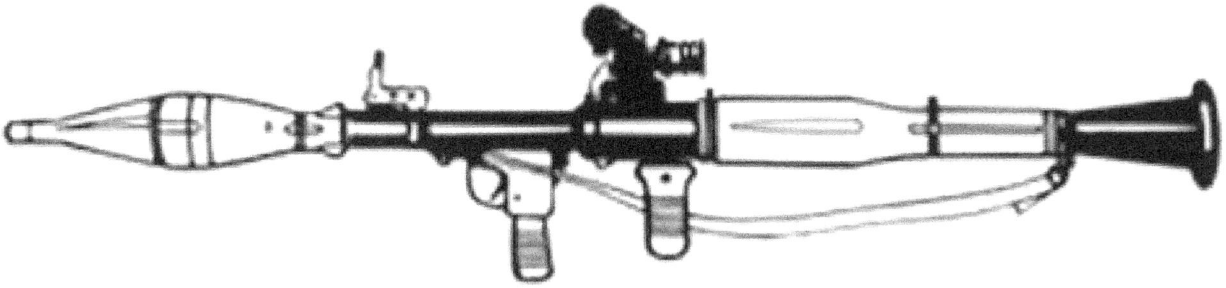

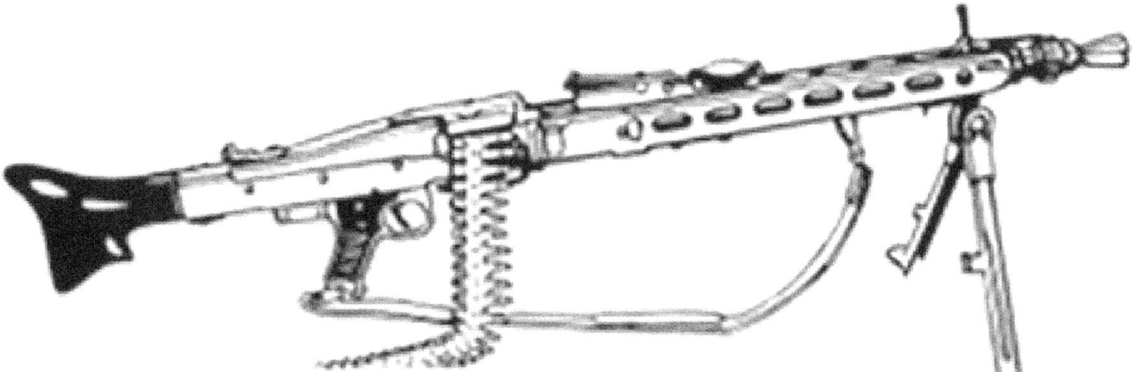

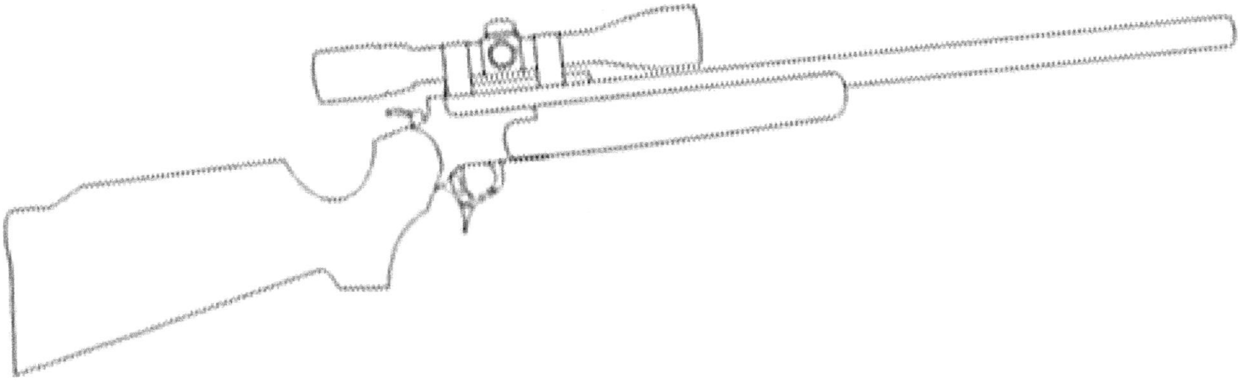

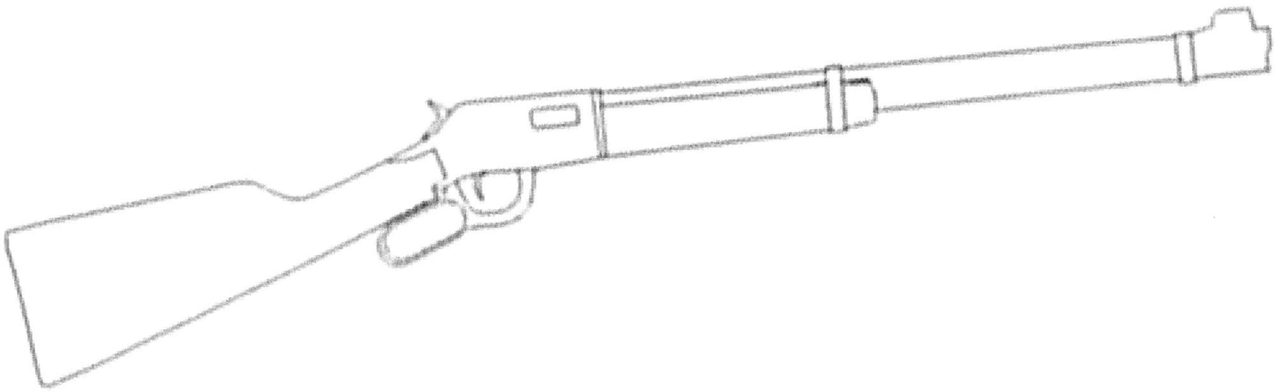

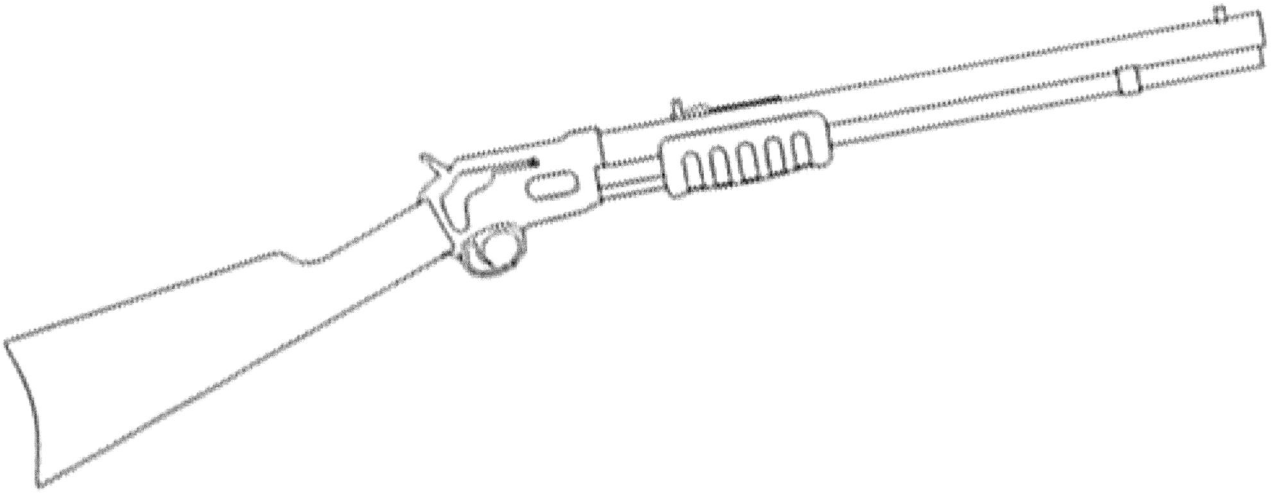

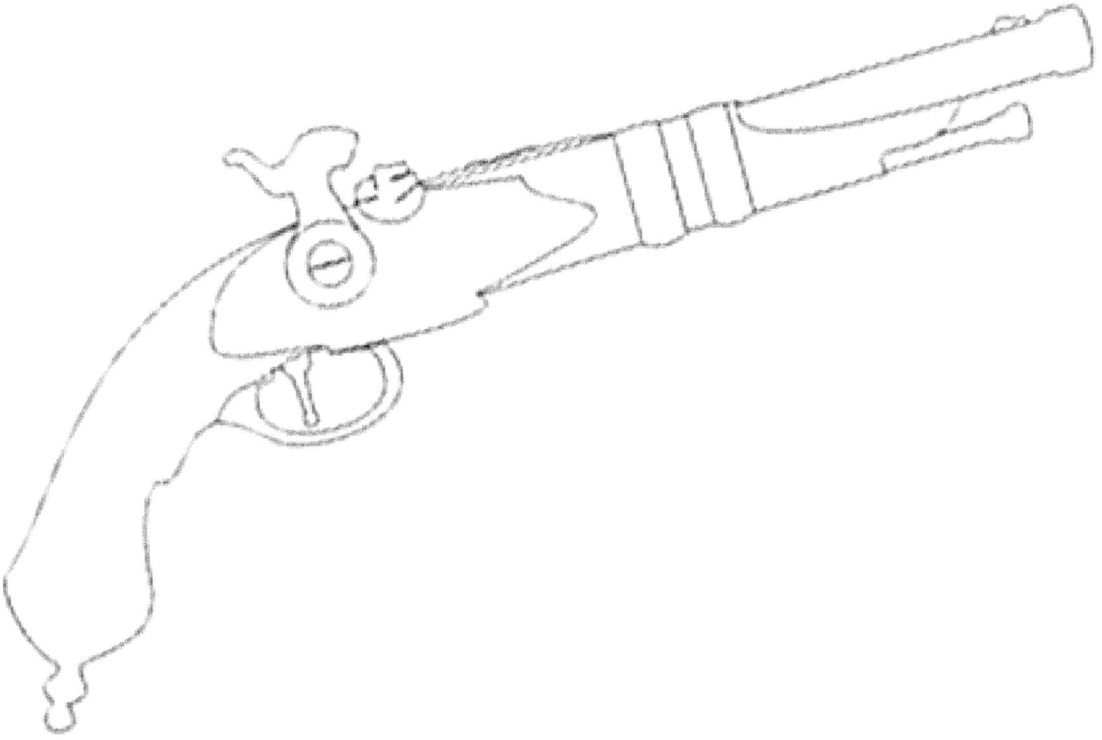

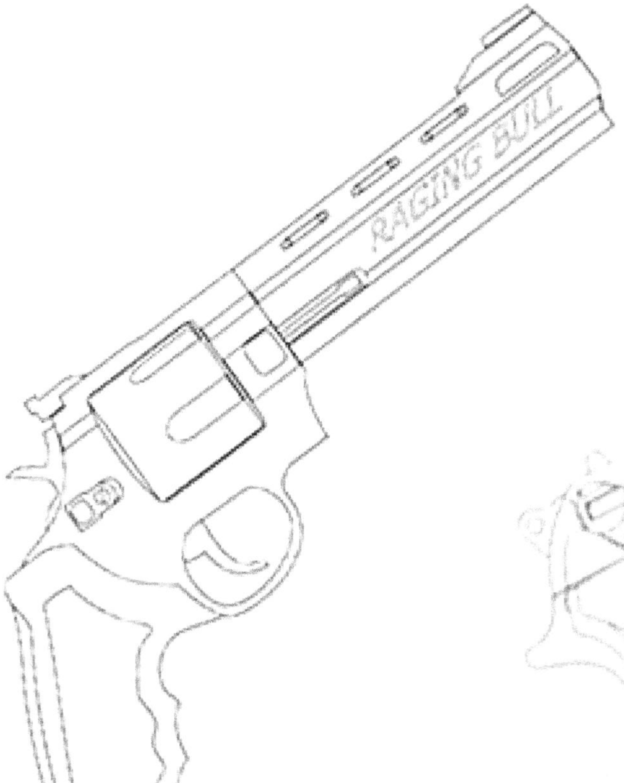
RAGING BULL

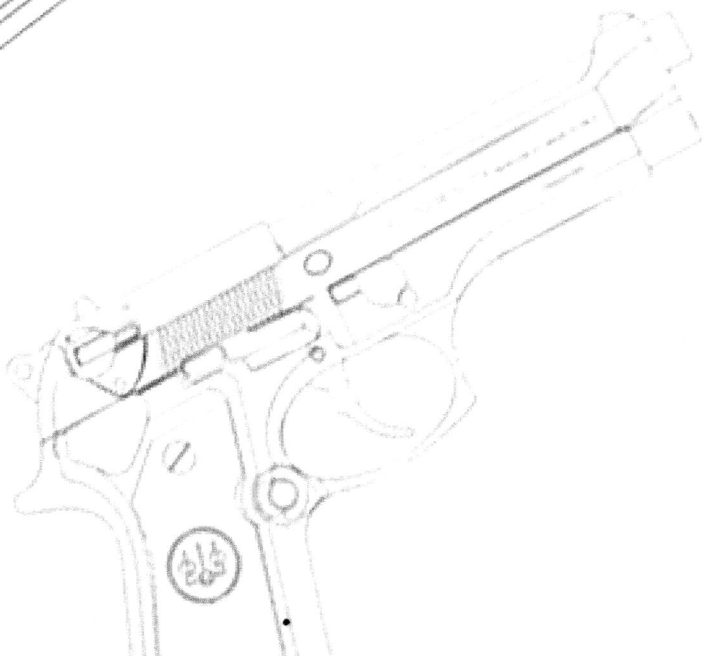

B6
F
B6
F
022

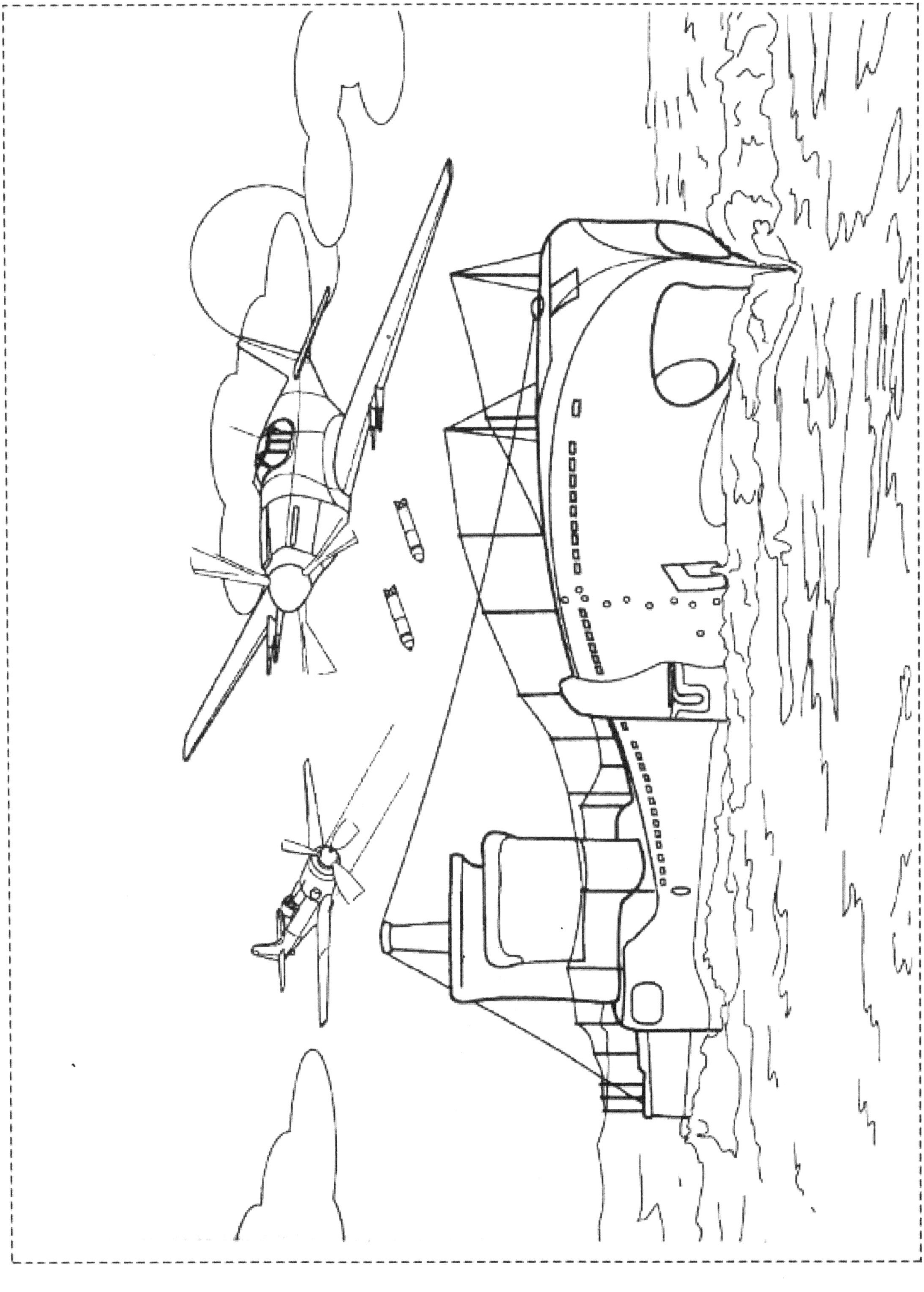

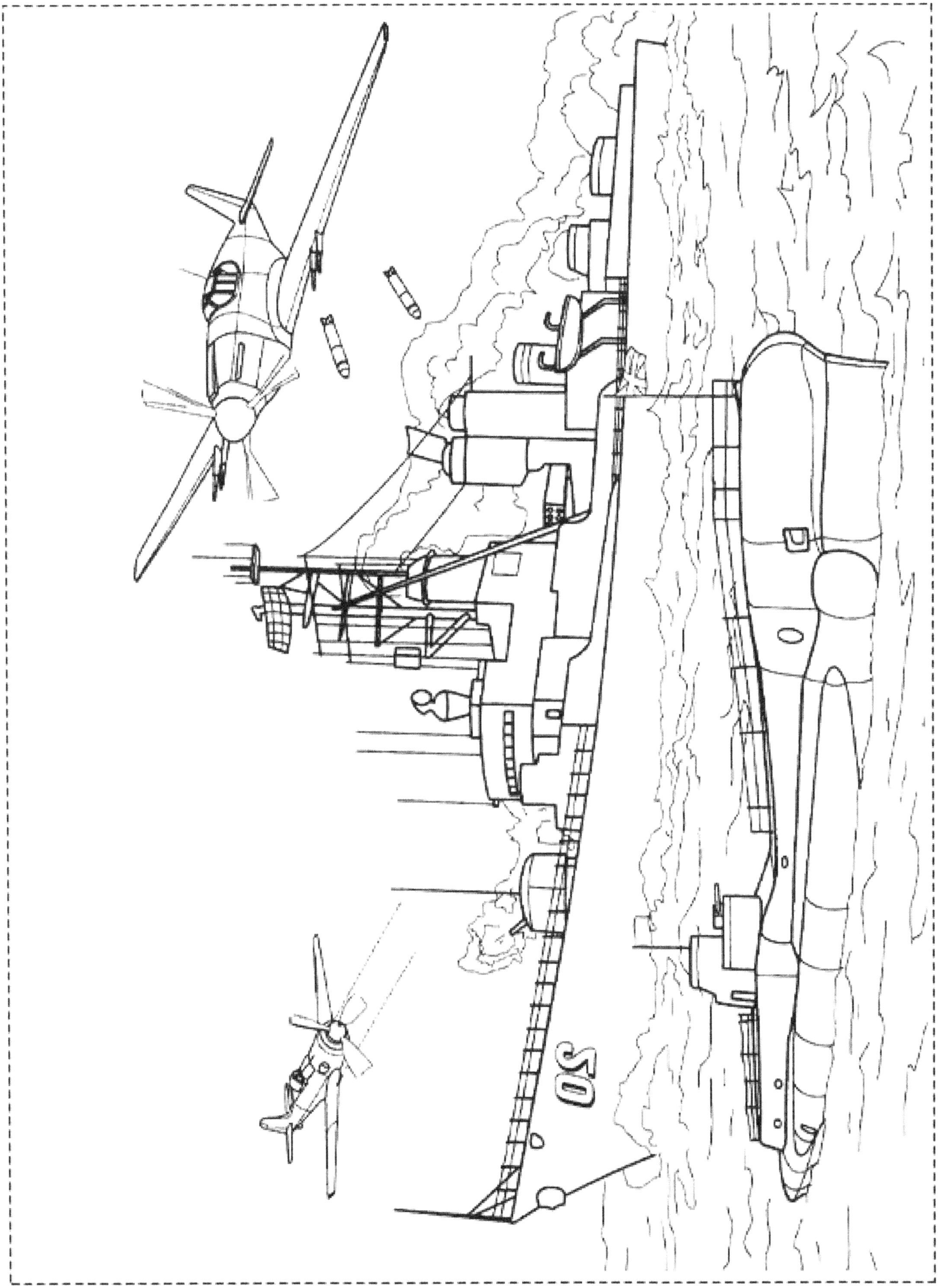
50

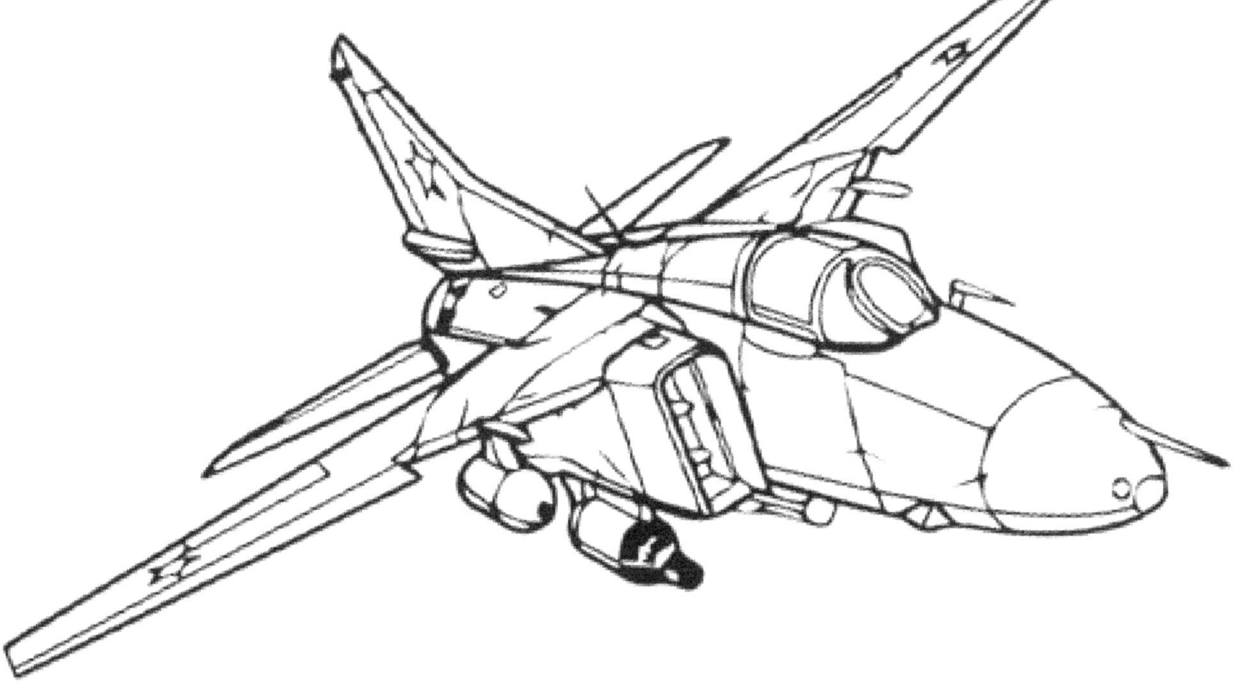

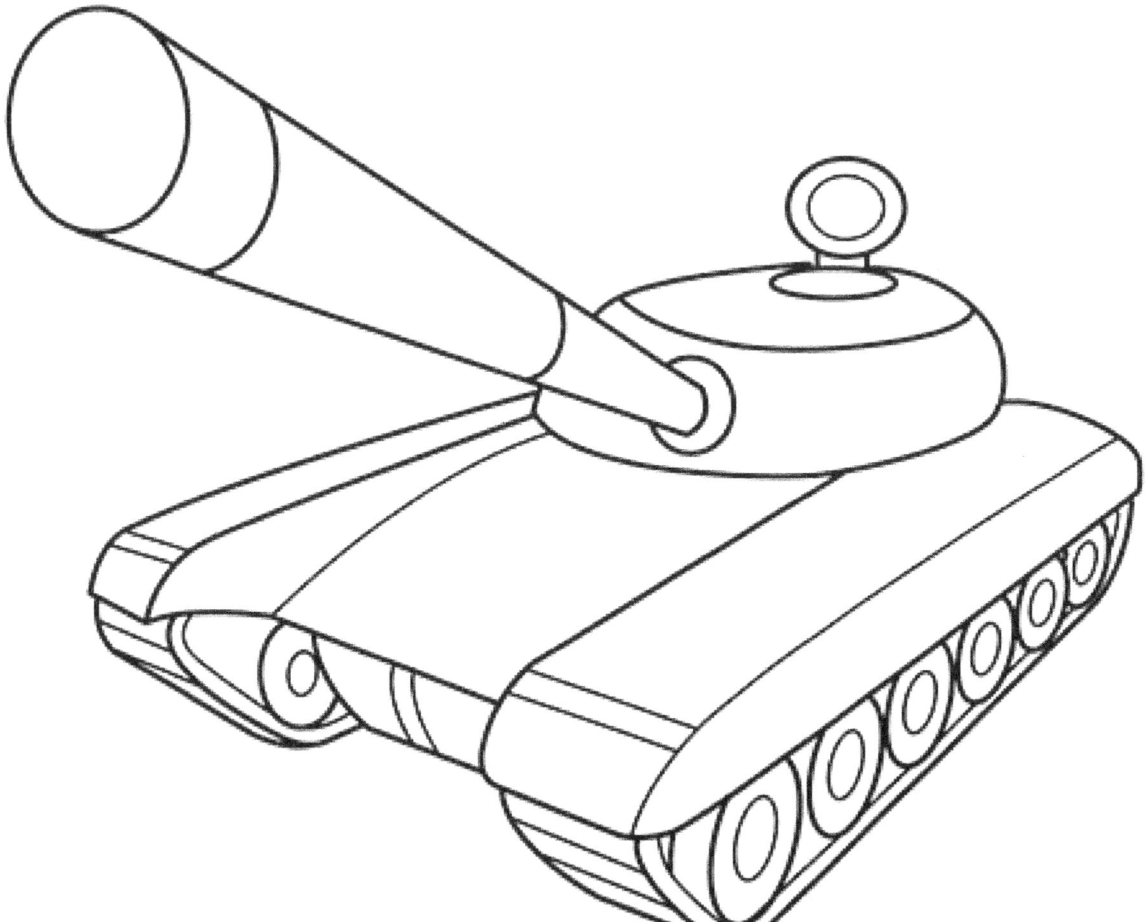

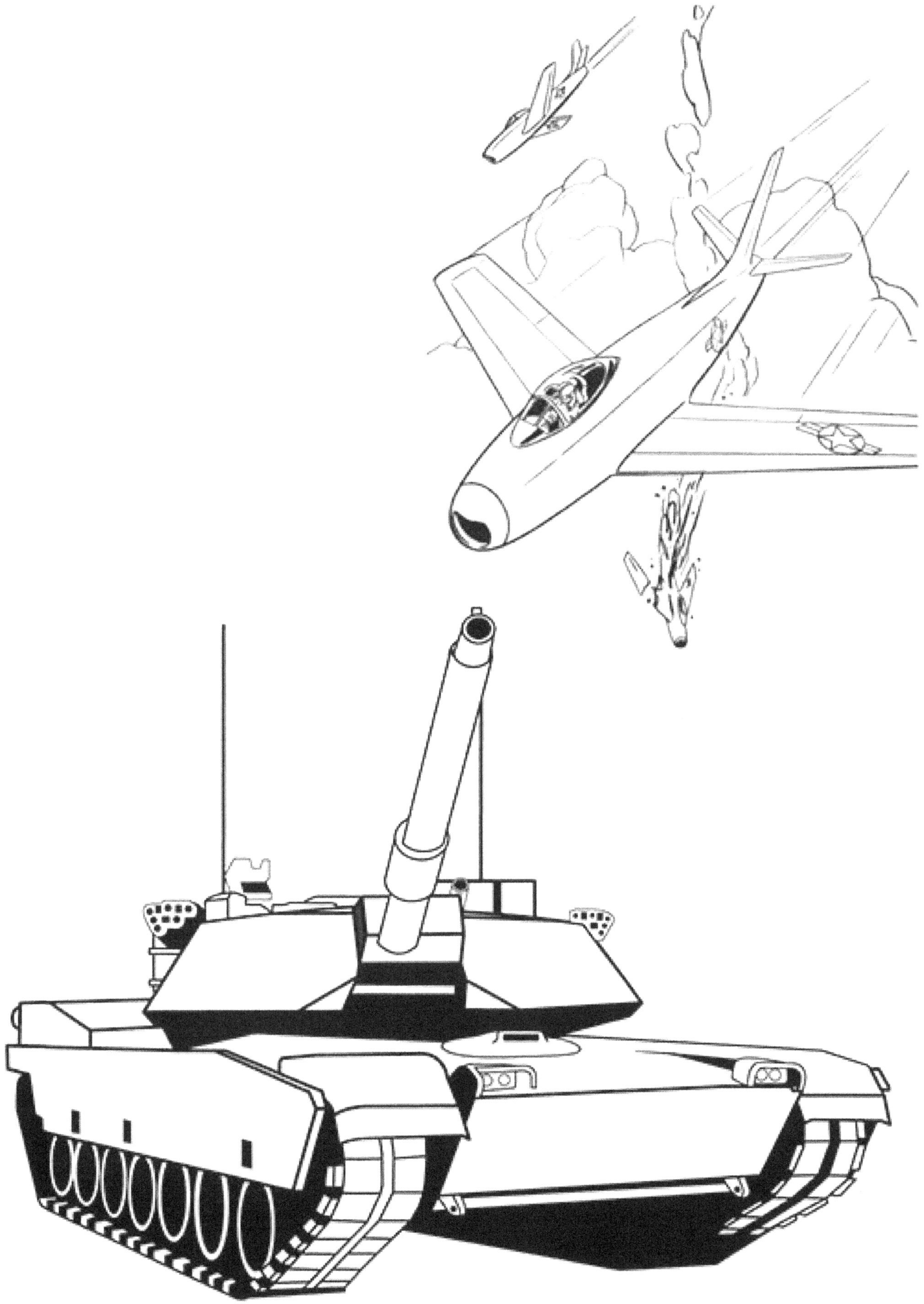

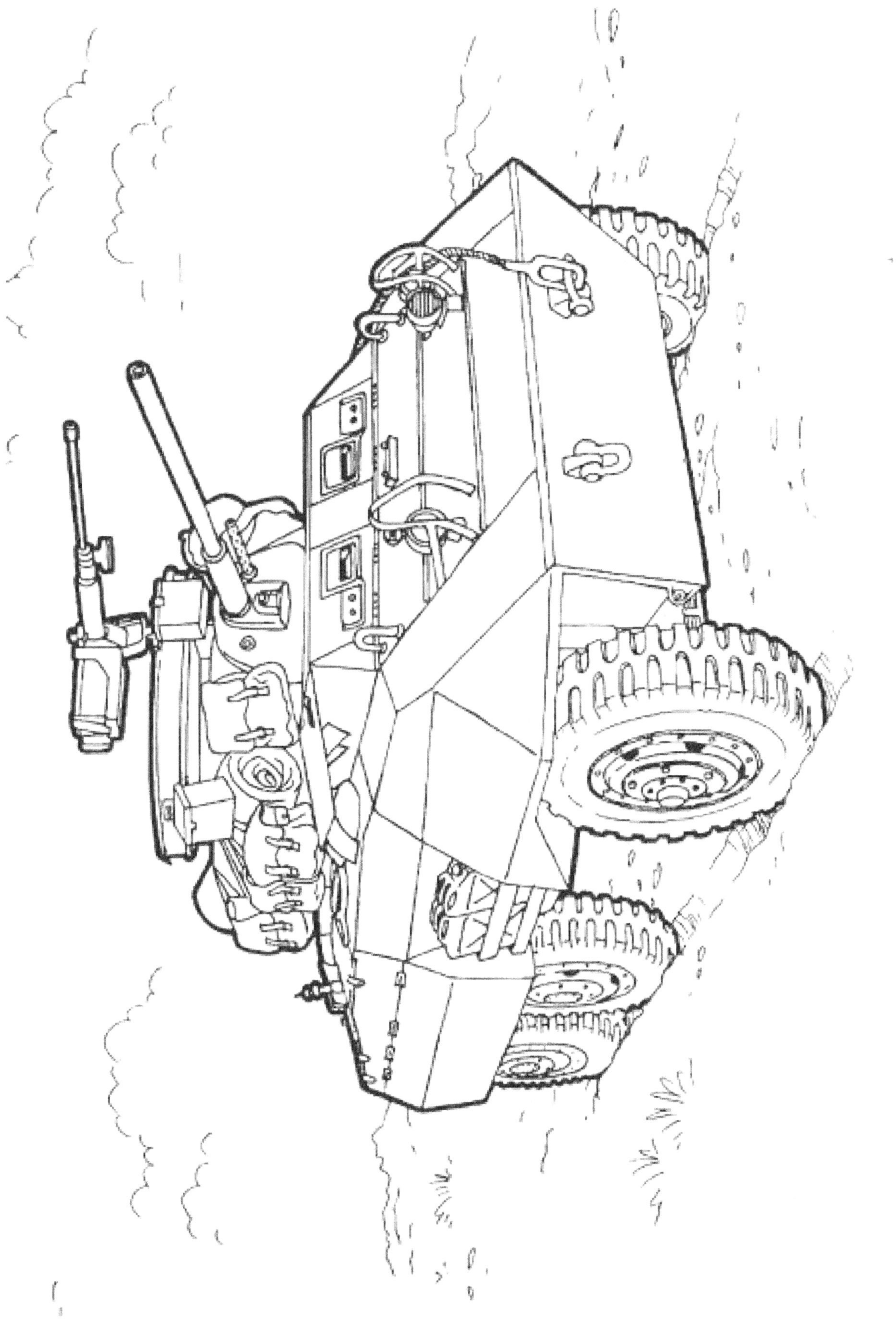

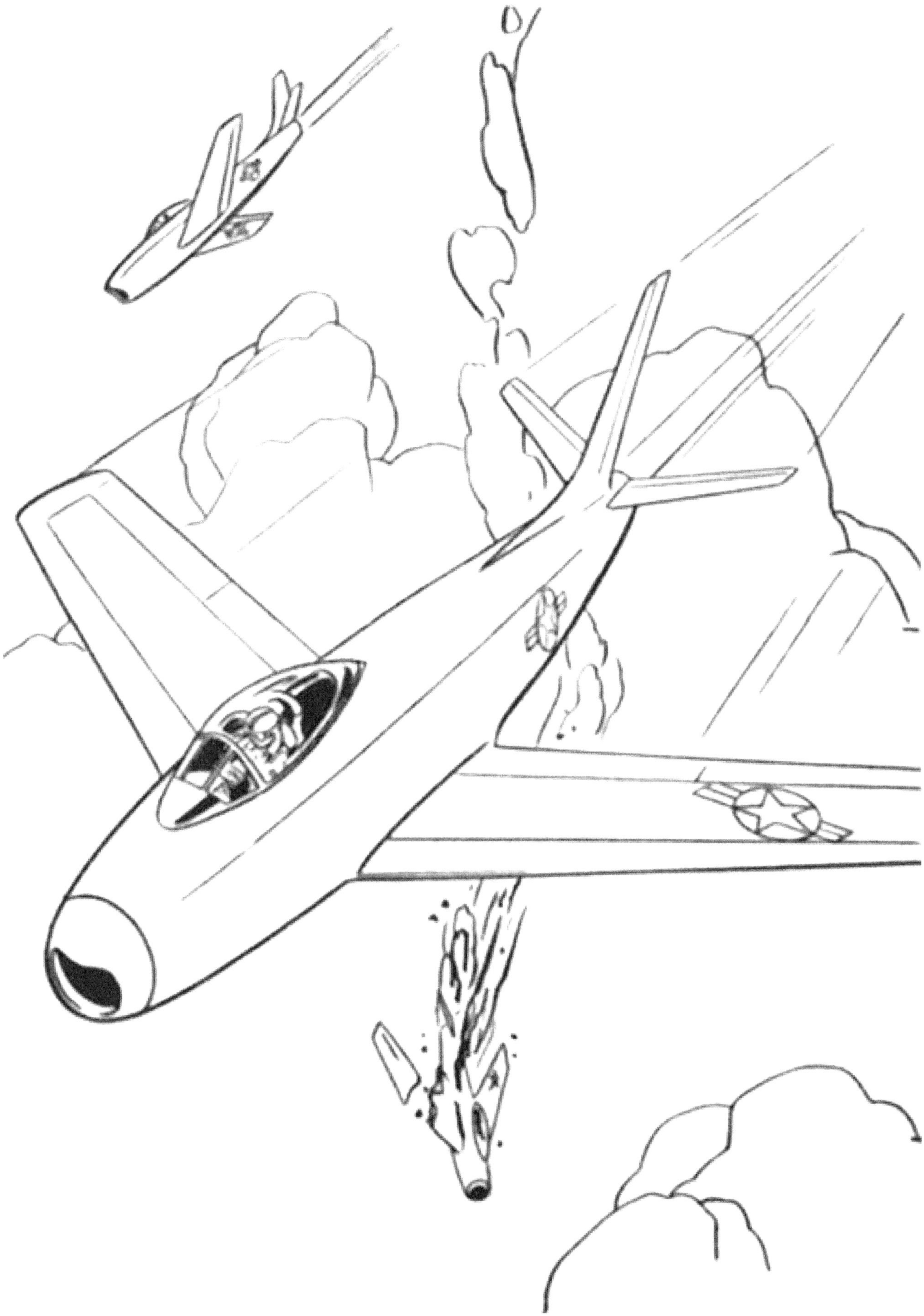

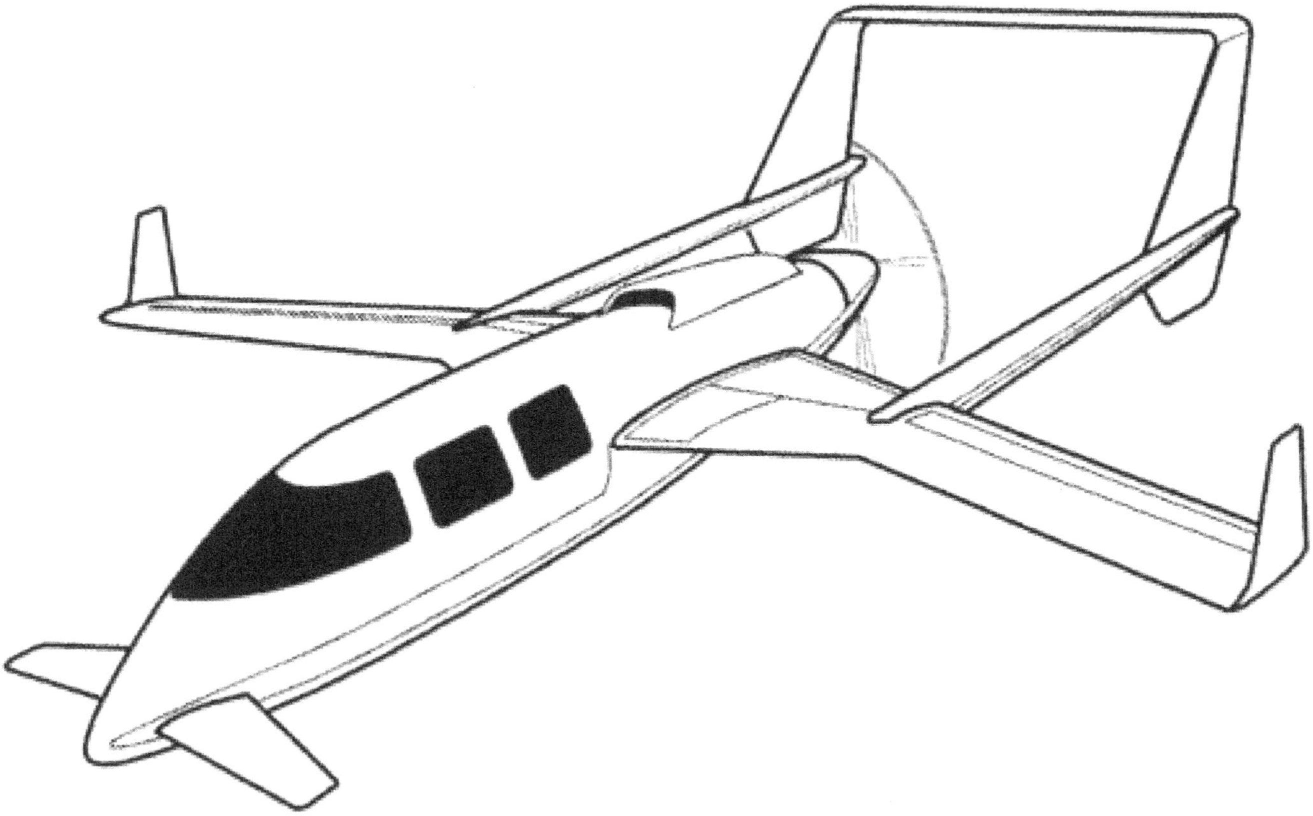

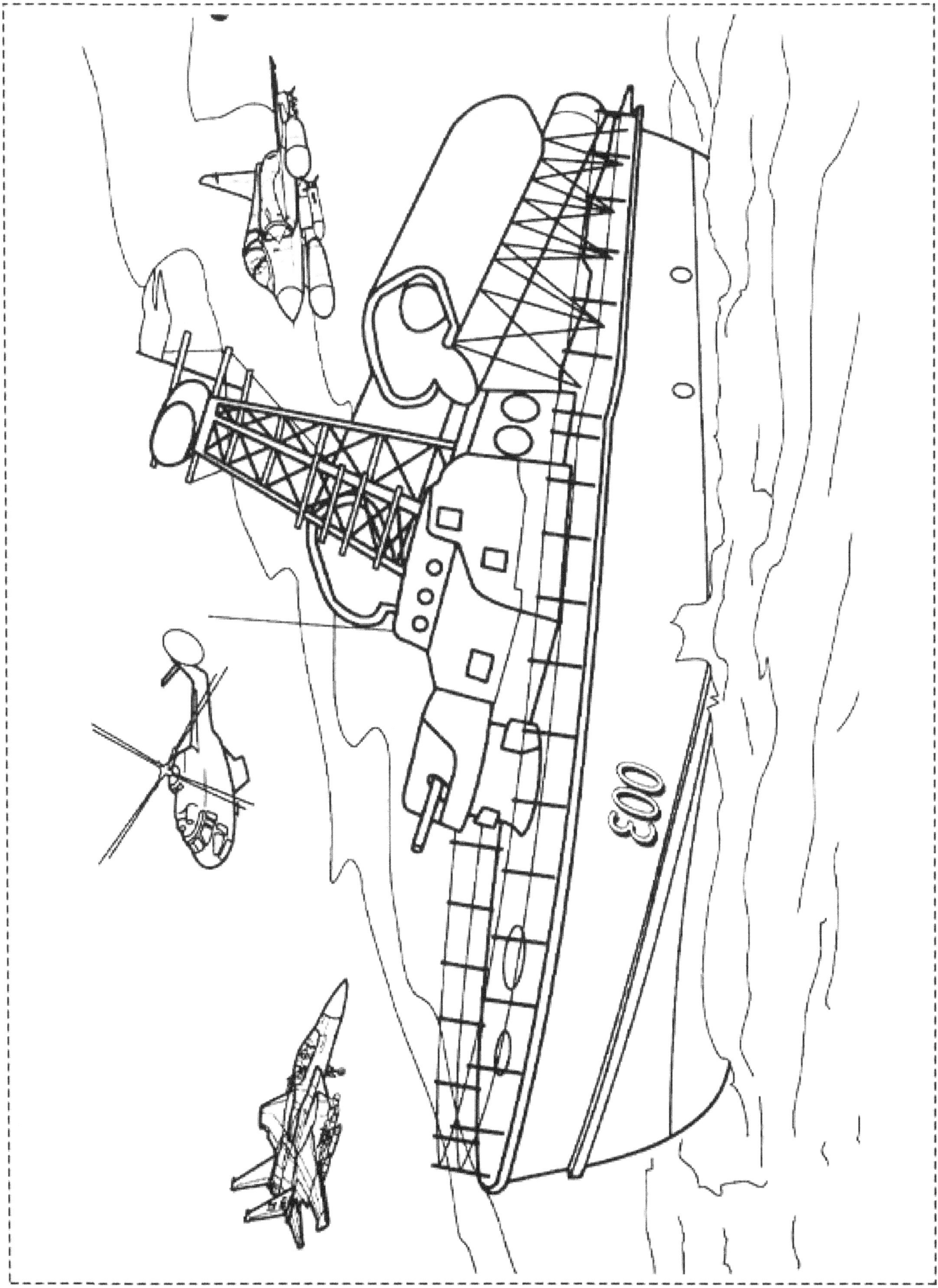
003

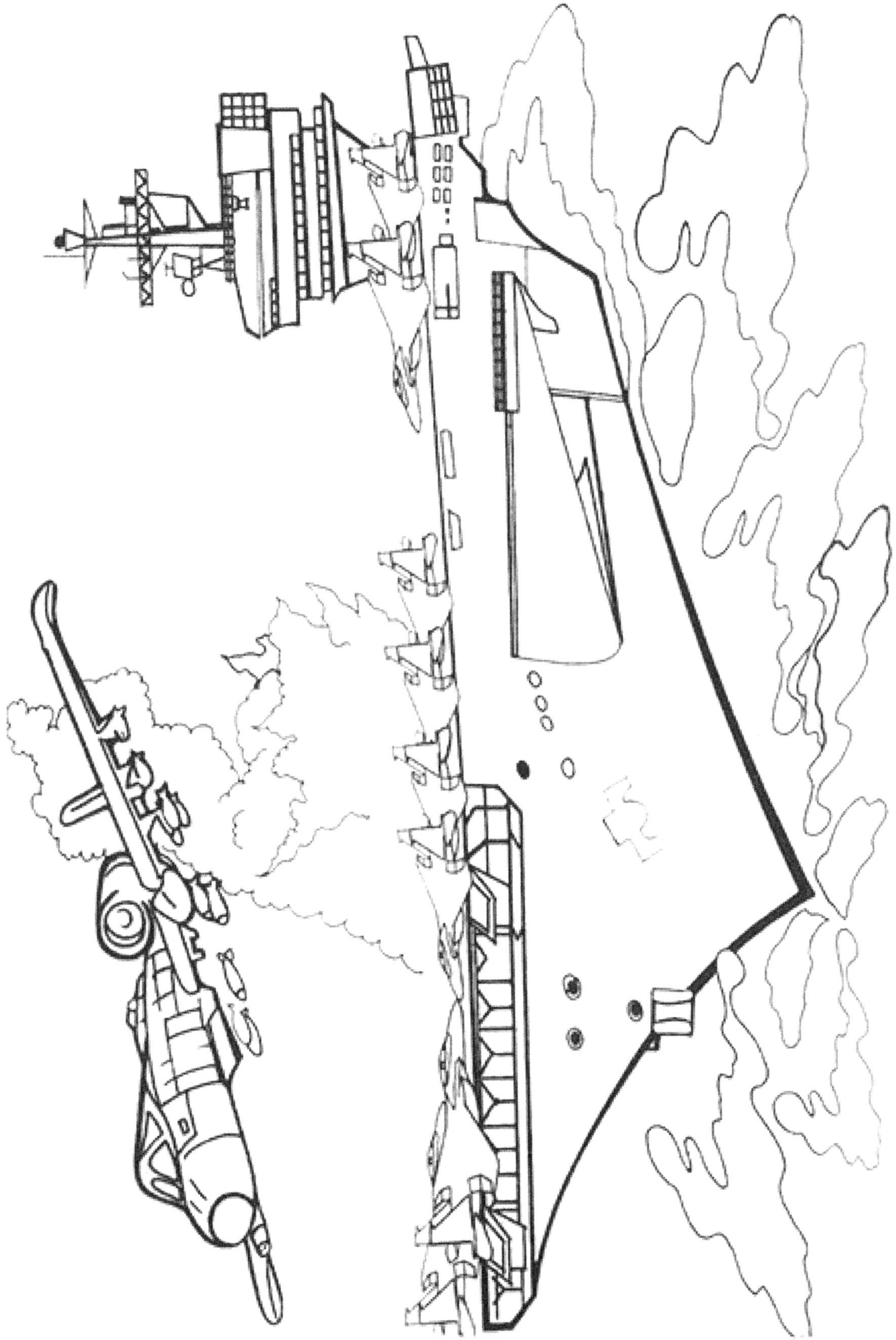

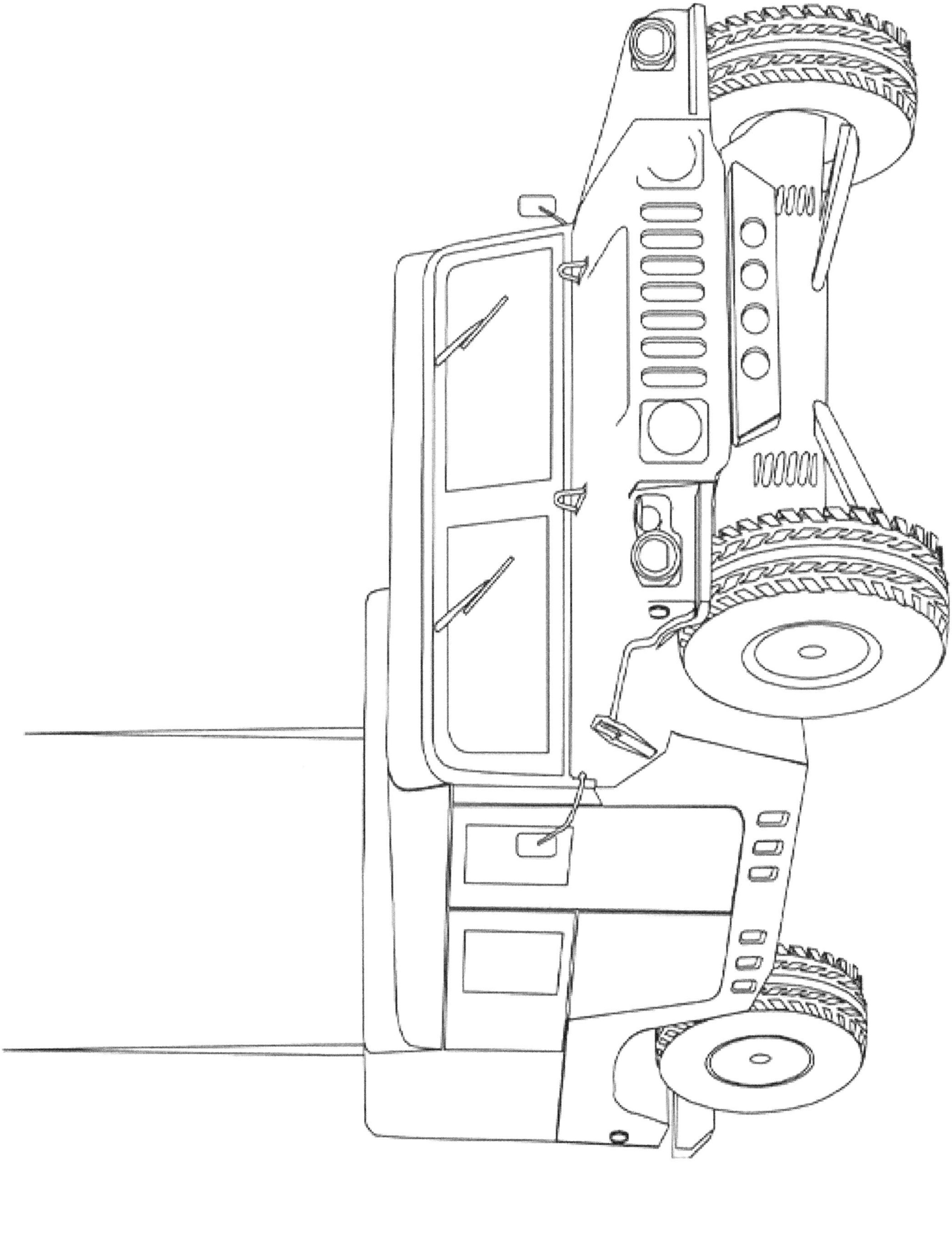

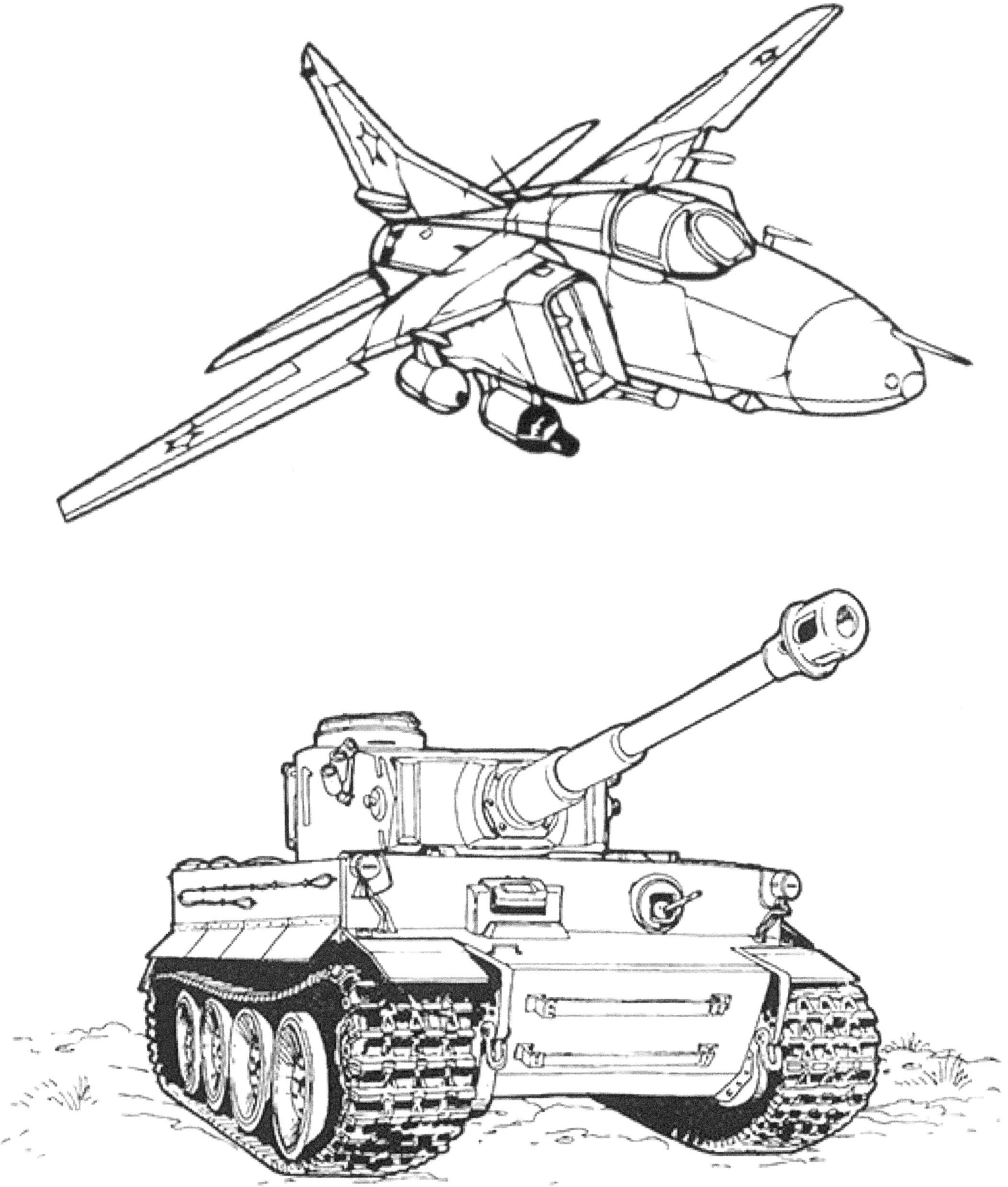

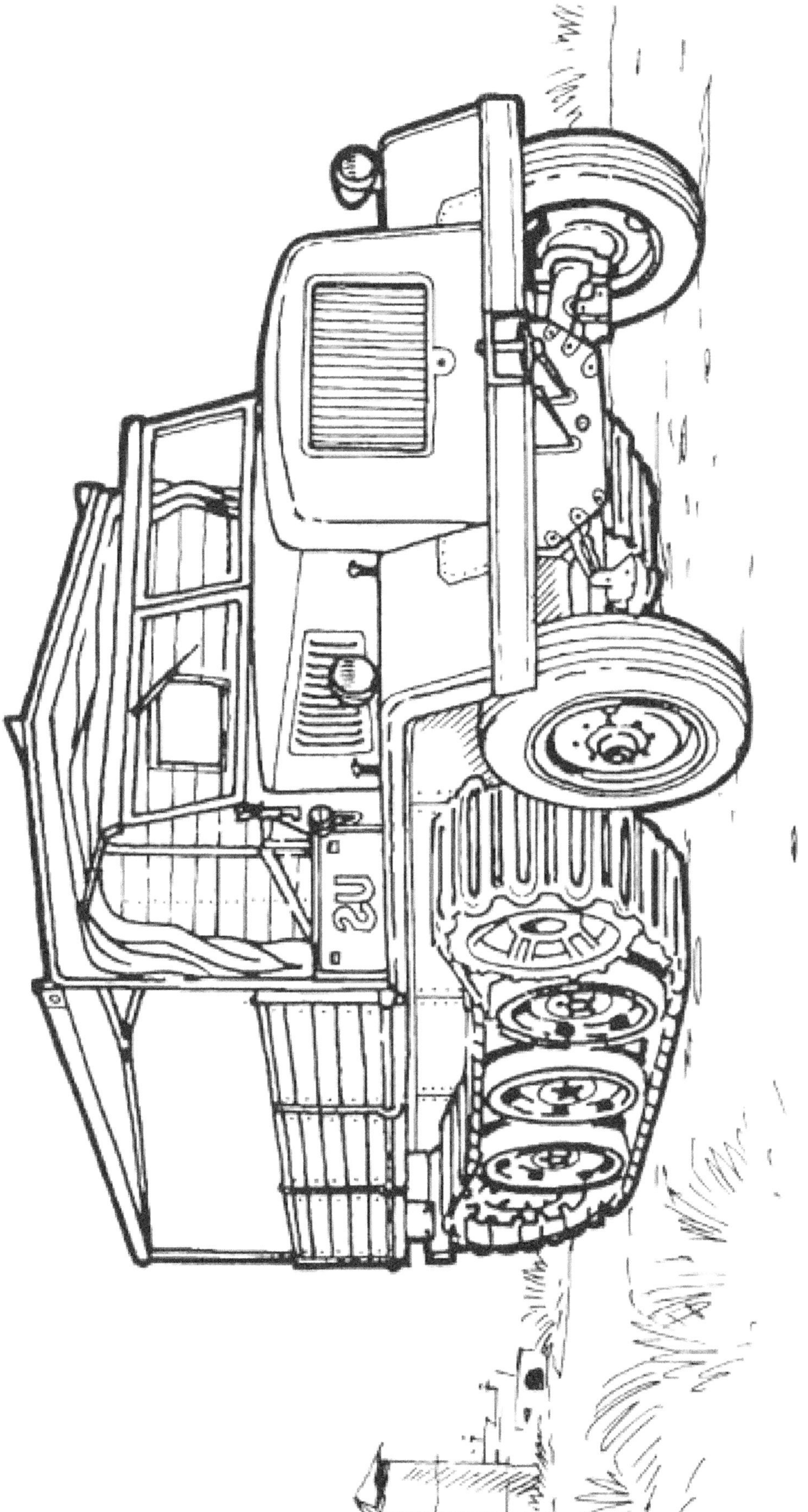

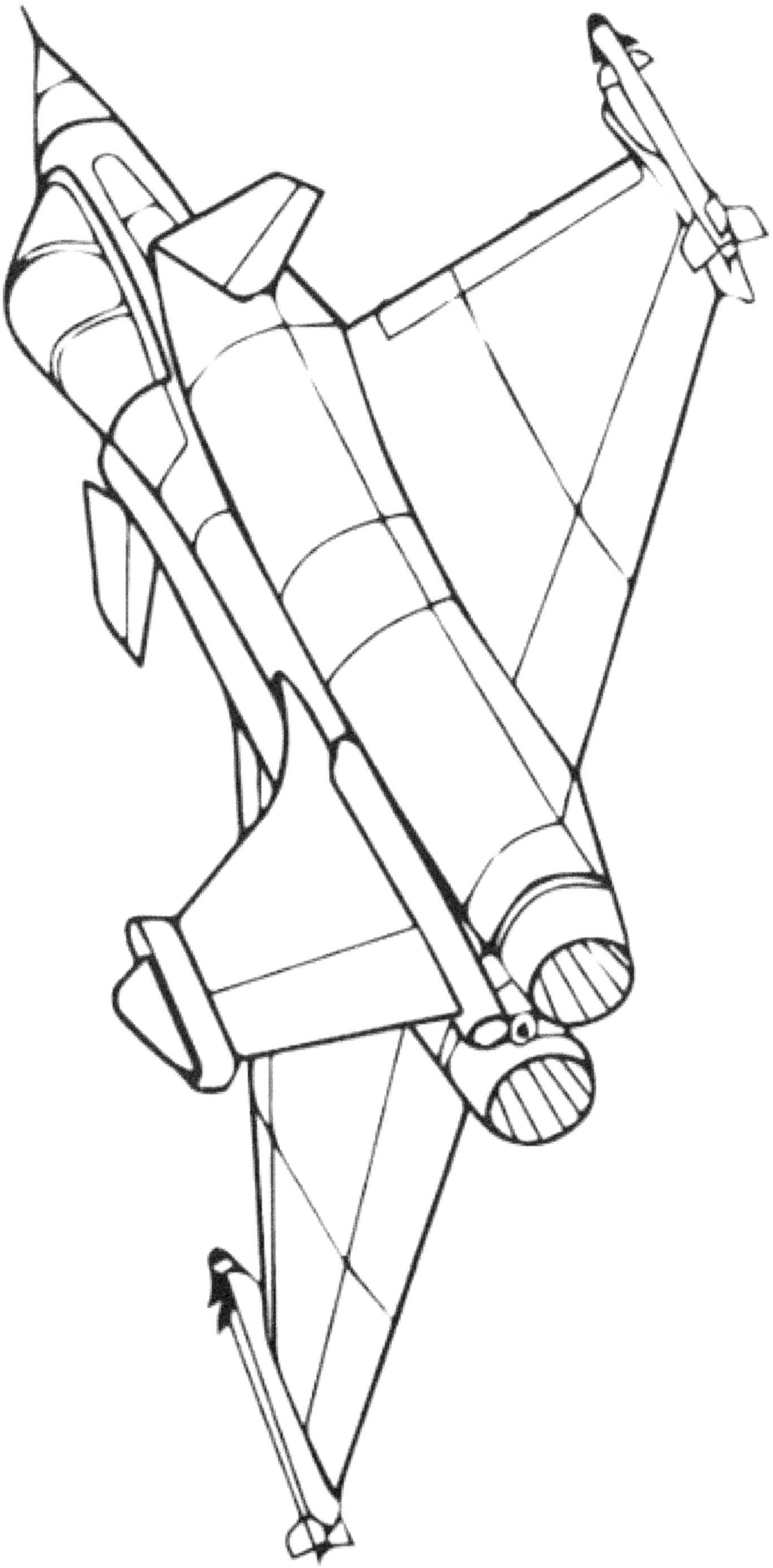

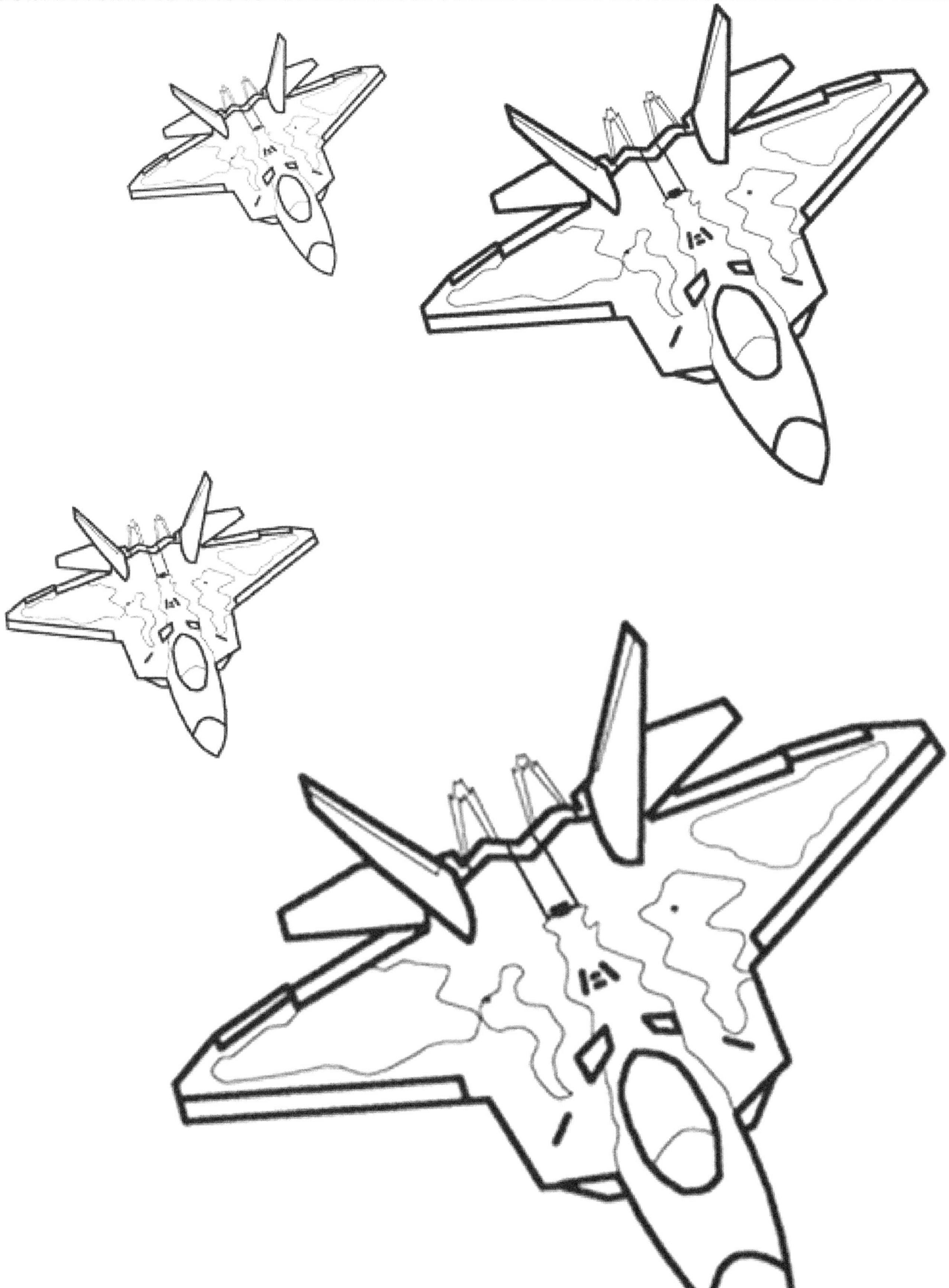

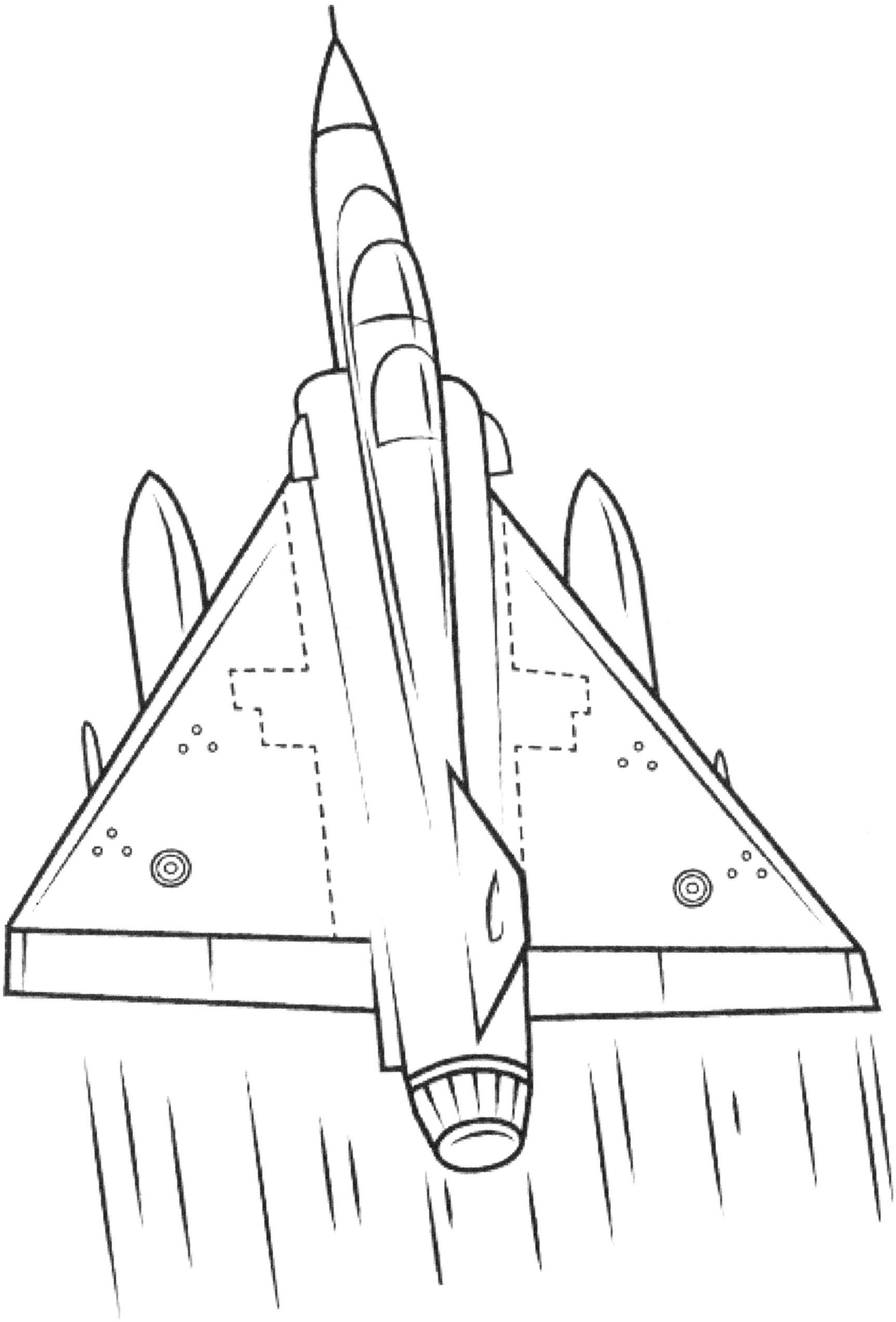

40

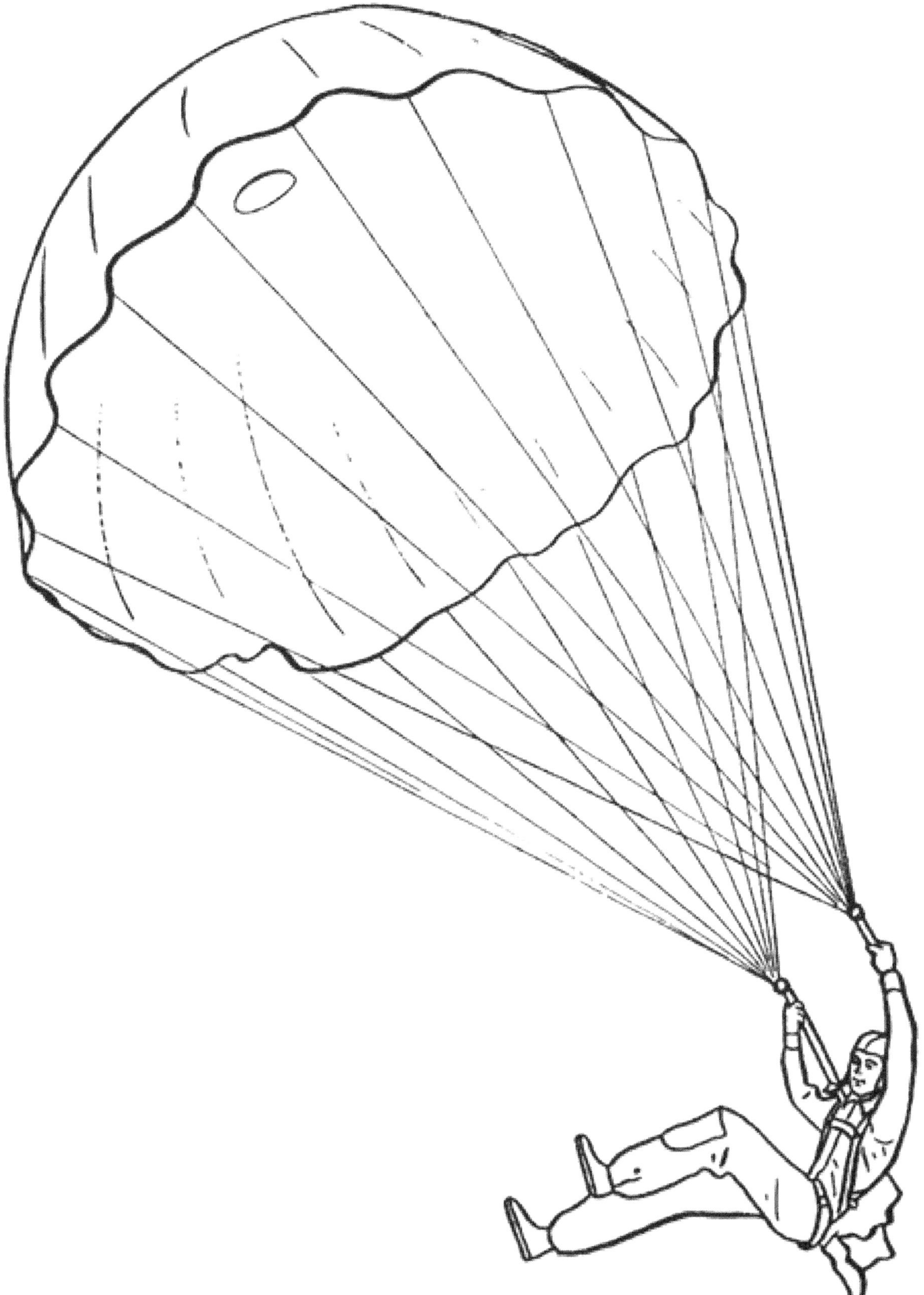

B6
F

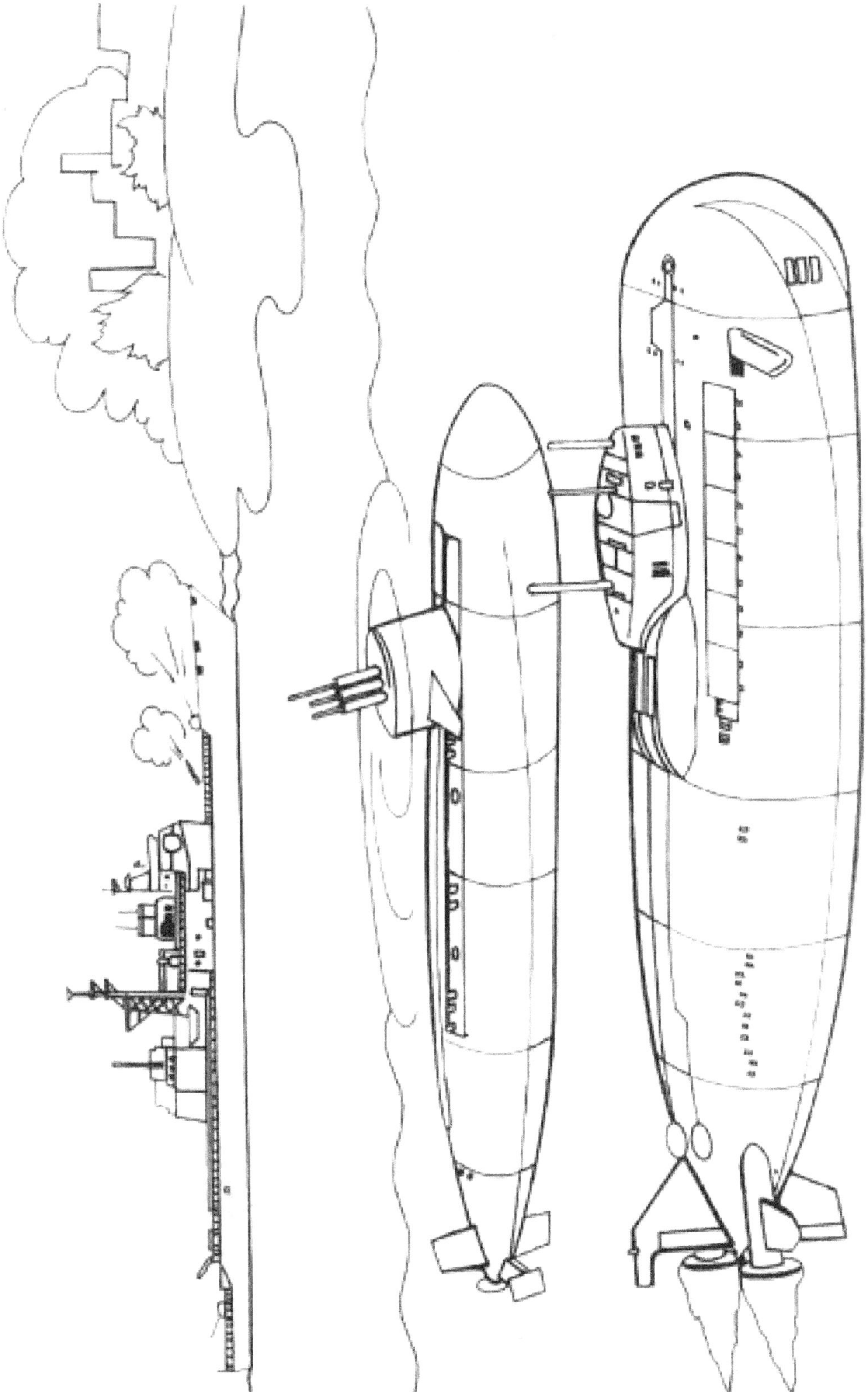

220
100

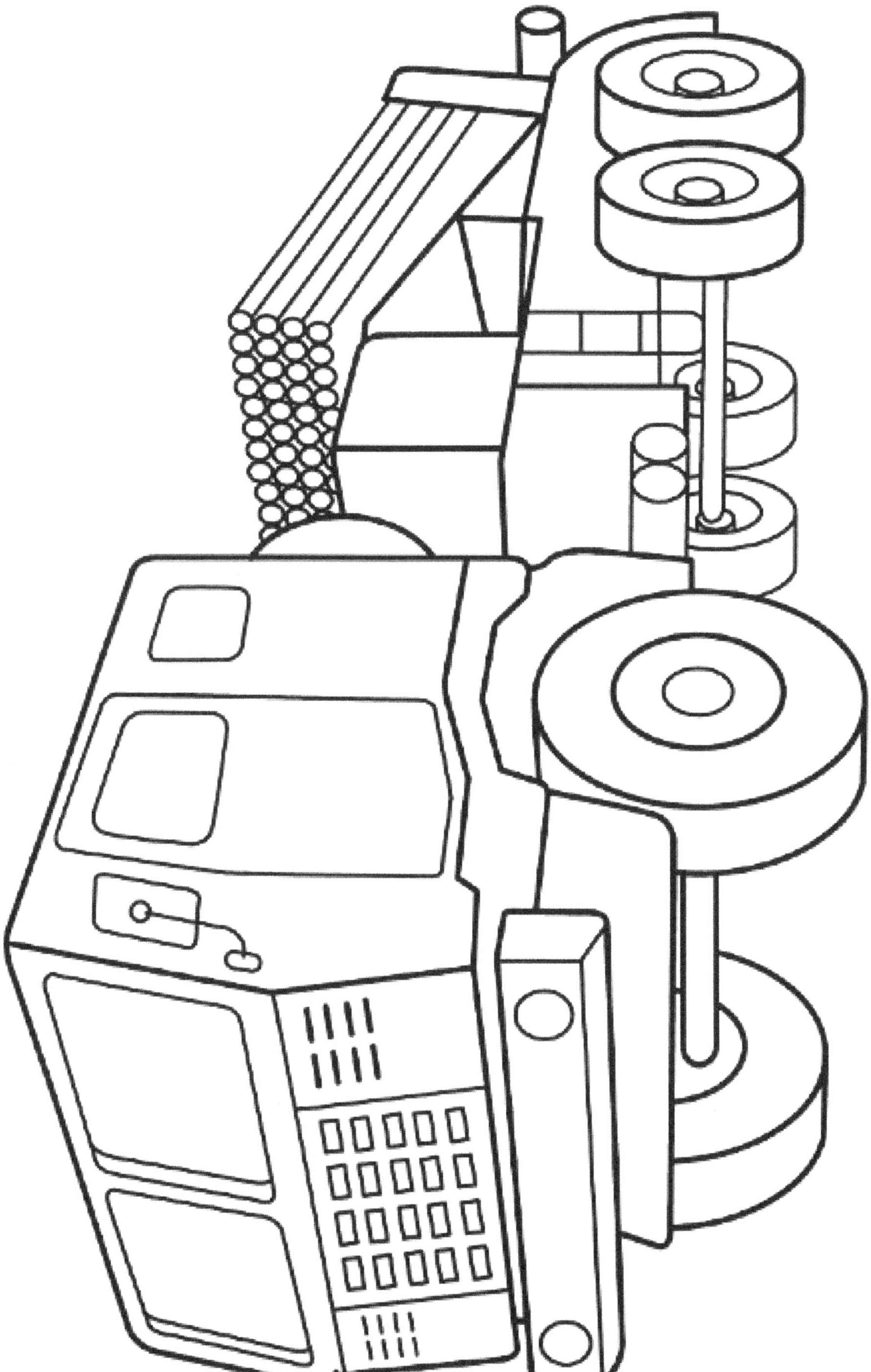

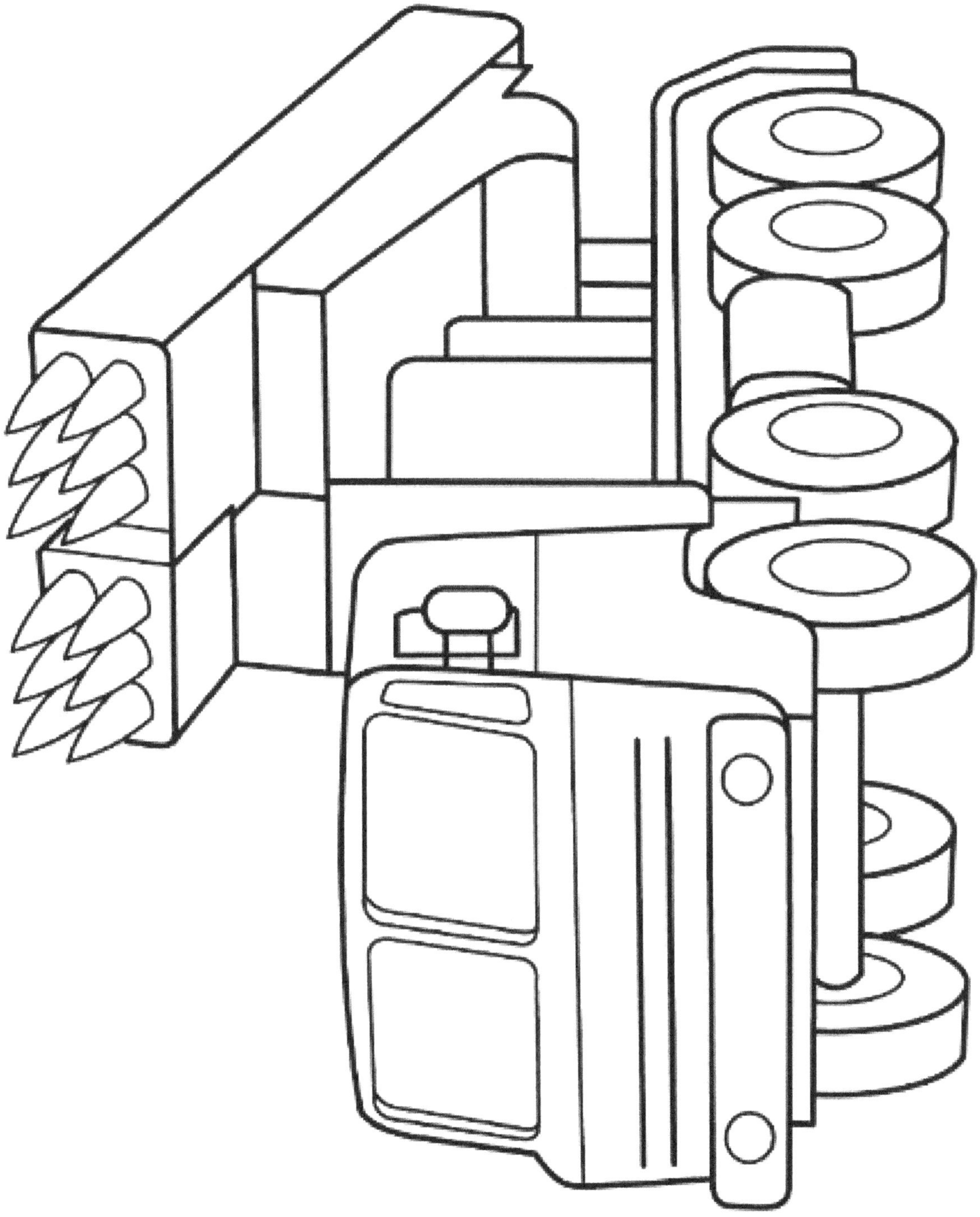

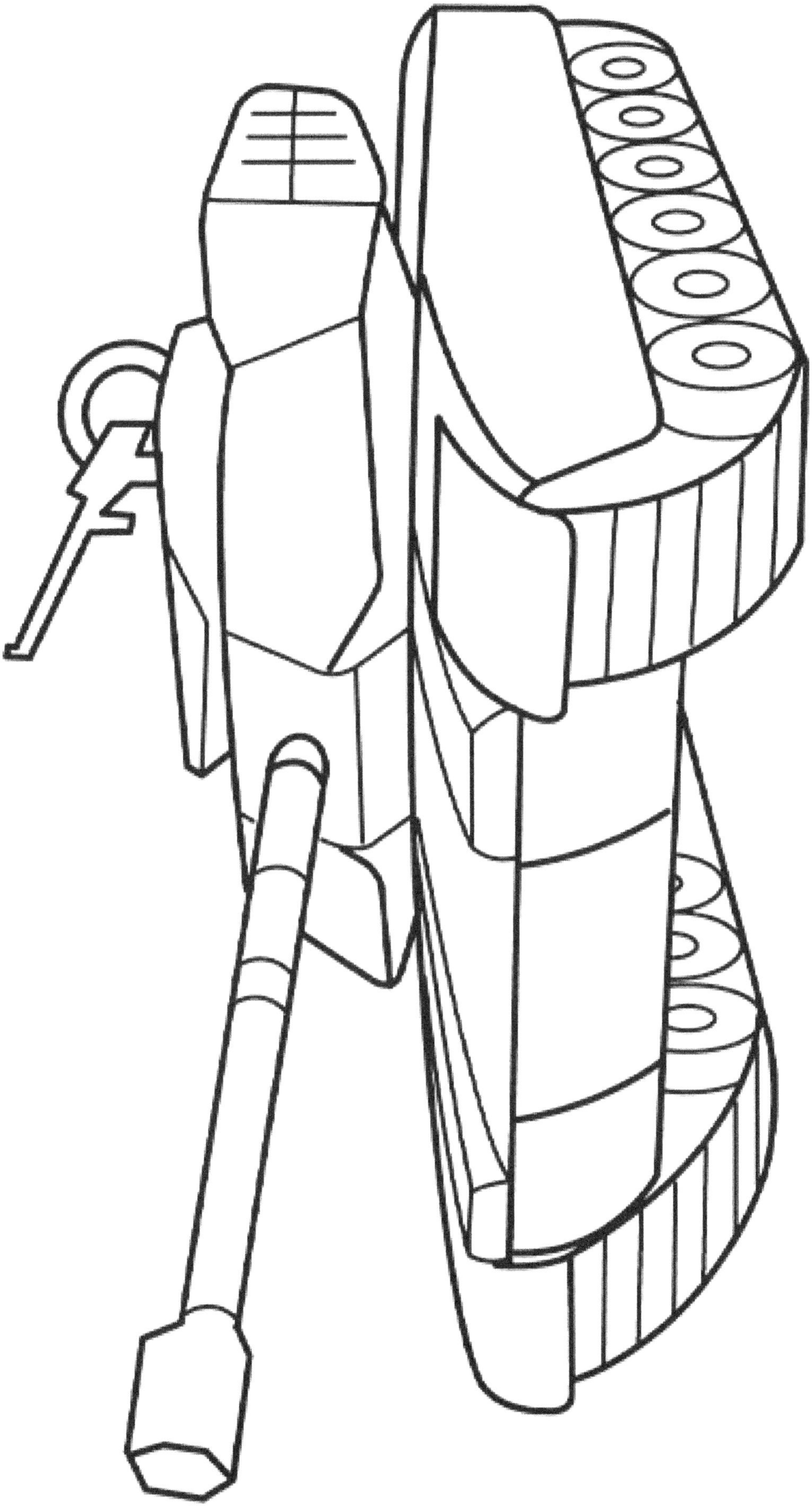

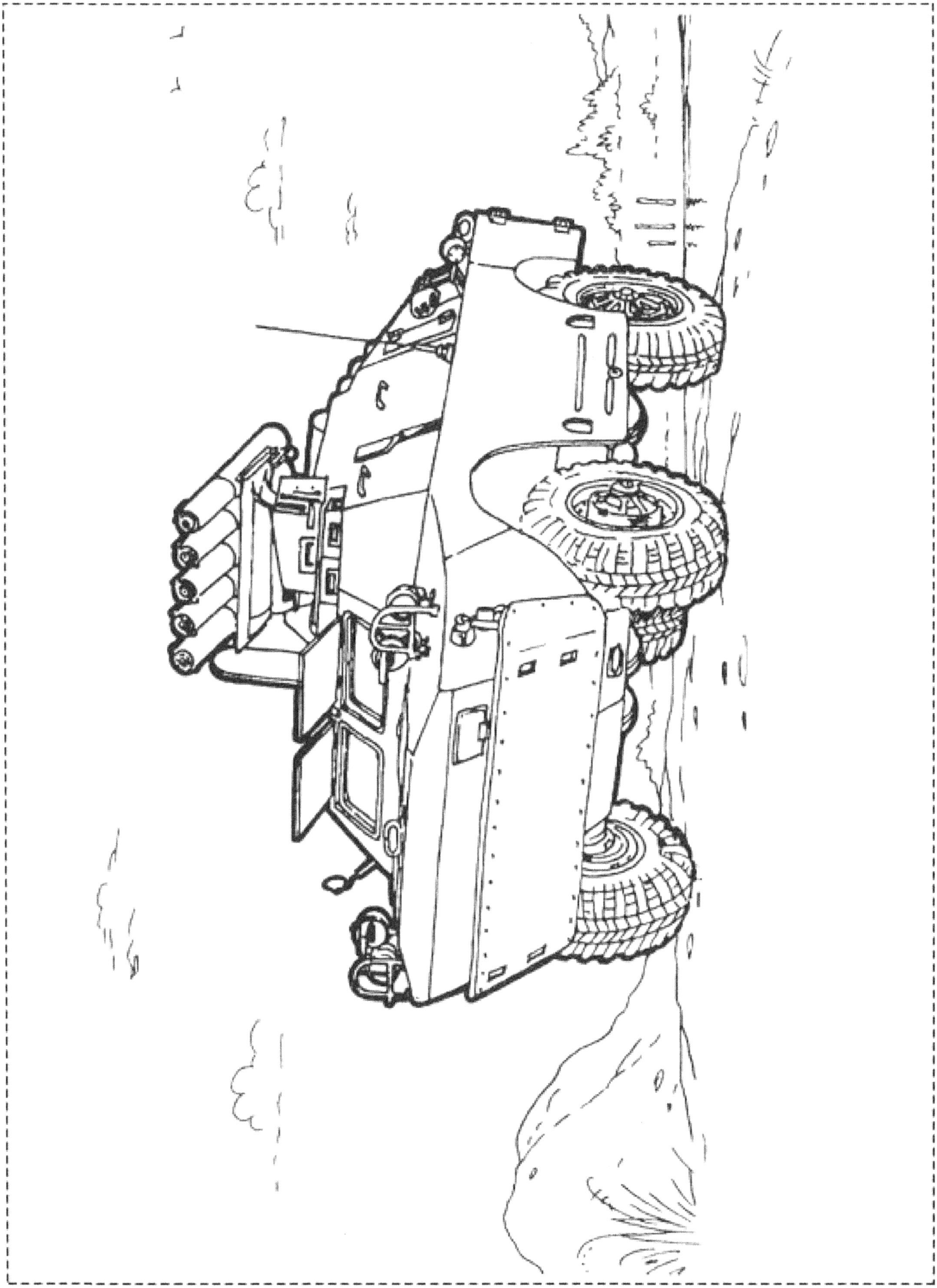

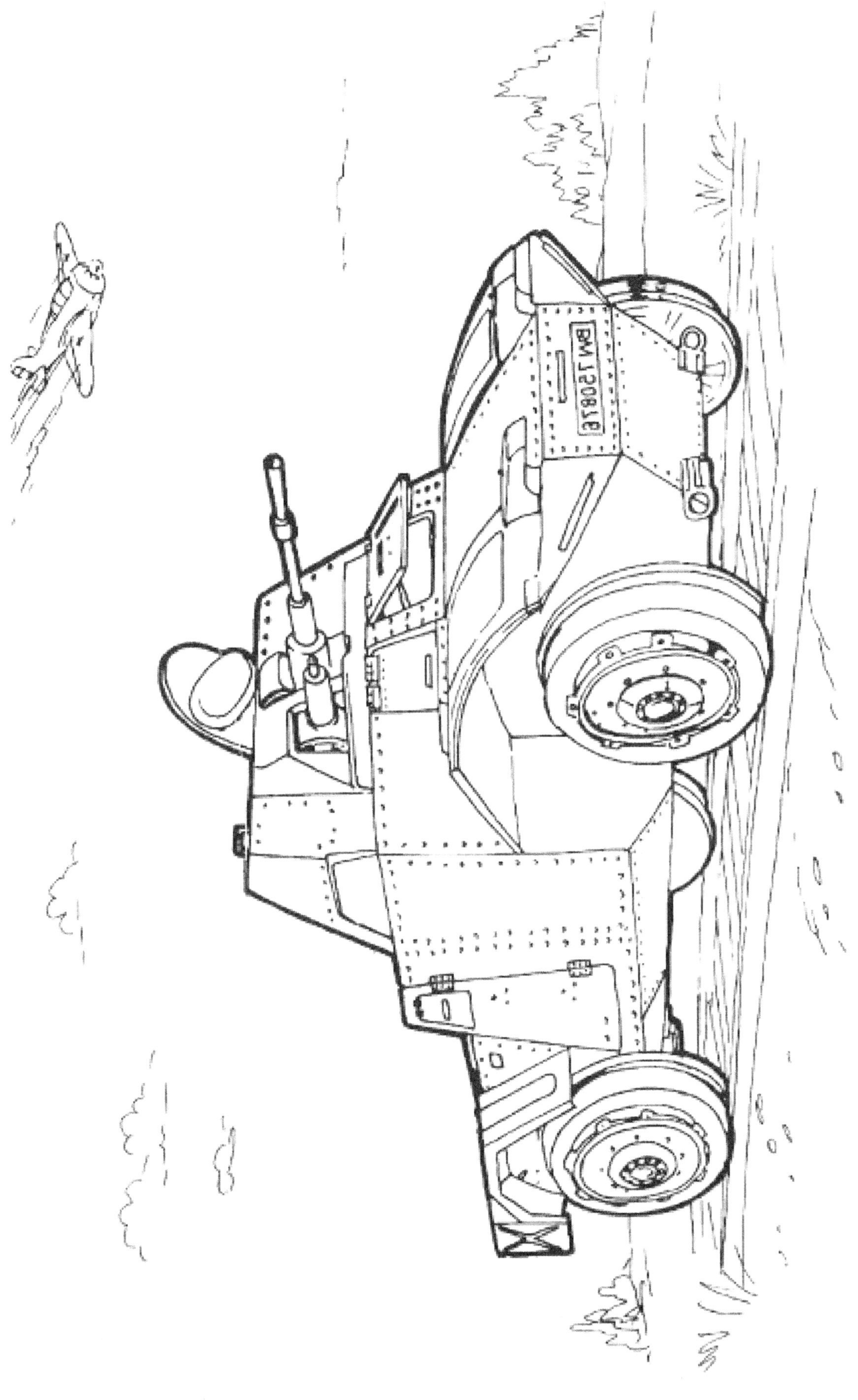

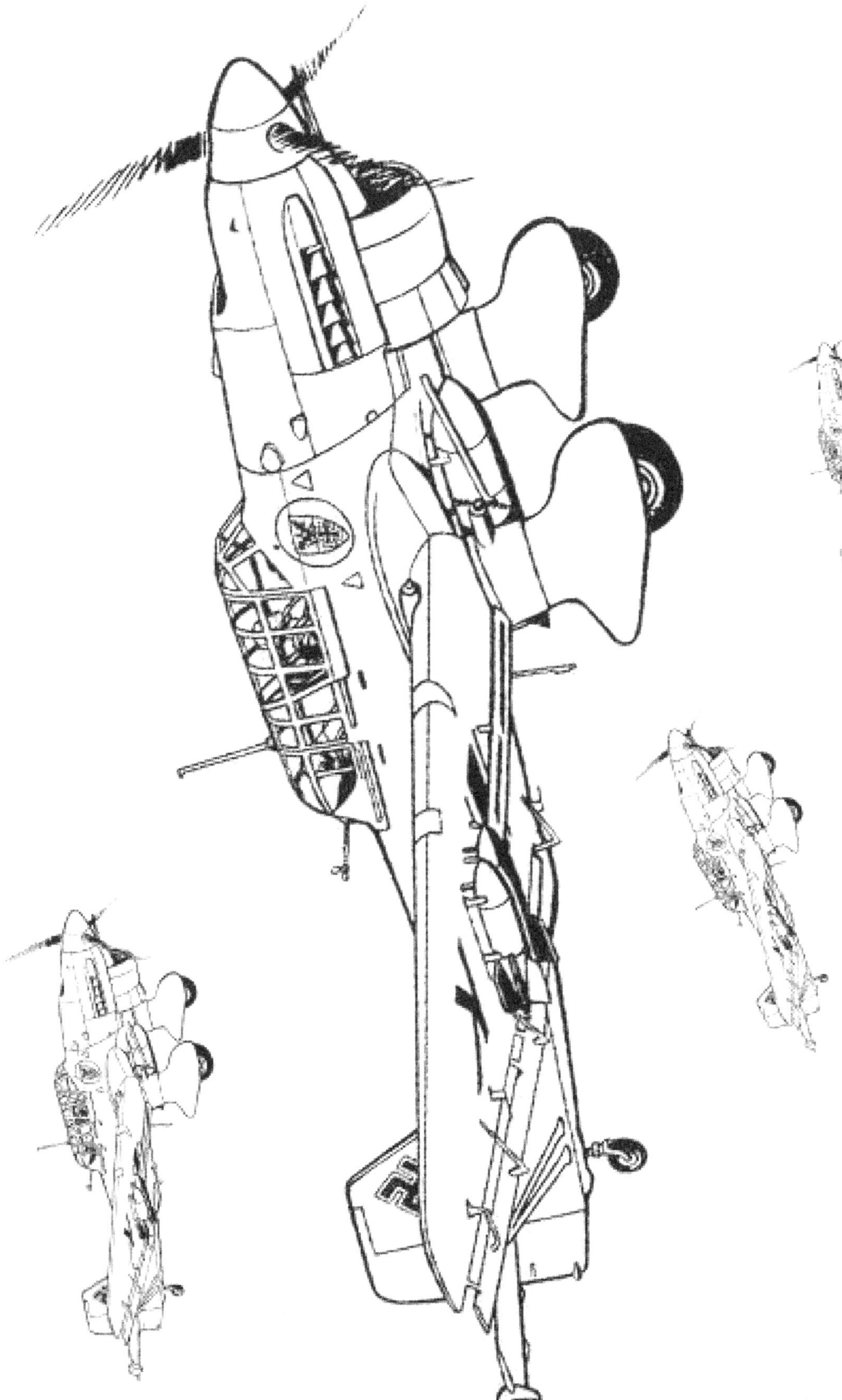

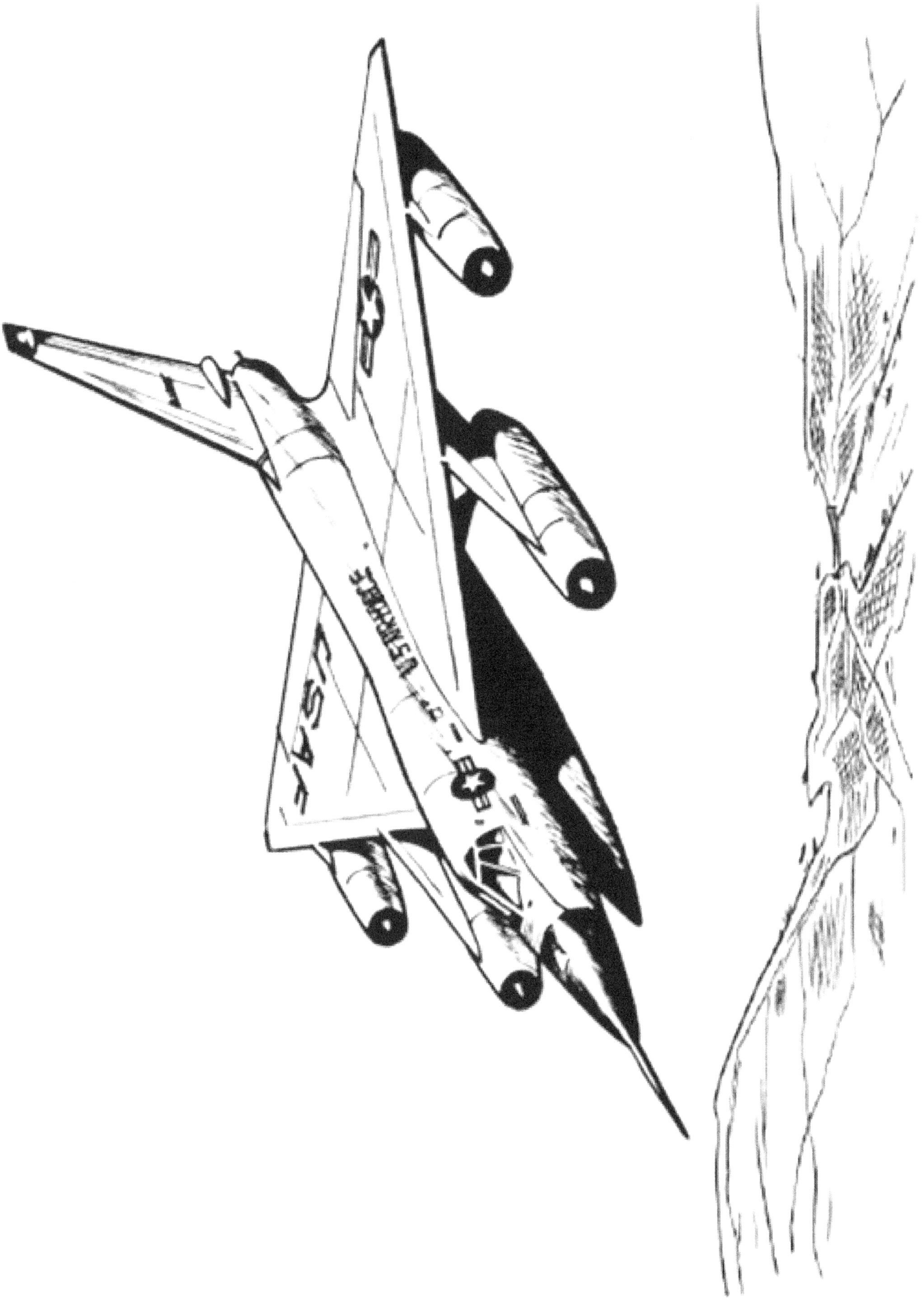
HUSTLER
USAF

Made in the USA
Monee, IL
16 November 2021

82245086R00057